HISTORY IN VERSE

KINGS & QUEENS of England 1066-2012

PAUL, BISHOP OF TRACHEIA

HISTORY IN VERSE

KINGS & QUEENS of England 1066-2012

G2 rights ltd

HISTORY IN VERSE
KINGS AND QUEENS OF ENGLAND 1066-2012

Copyright ©Paul, Bishop of Tracheia 2012

First edition published in the UK in December 2012
© G2 Rights Limited 2012
www.G2rights.co.uk

All rights reserved. No part of this work may be reproduced or utilised in any form or by any means, electronic or mechanical, including photocopying, recording or by any information storage and retrieval system, without prior written permission of the publisher.

Print Edition ISBN: 978-1-78281-004-9

The views in this book are those of the author but they are general views only and readers are urged to consult the relevant and qualified specialist for individual advice in particular situations. G2 Rights Limited hereby exclude all liability to the extent permitted by law of any errors or omissions in this book and for any loss, damage or expense (whether direct or indirect) suffered by a third party relying on any information contained in this book. All our best endeavours have been made to secure copyright clearance but in the event of any copyright owner being overlooked please go to www.G2rights.co.uk where you will find all relevant contact information.

G2 Rights Ltd, Unit 9 Whiffens Farm, Clement Street, Hextable, Kent, BR8 7PG

BY THE SAME AUTHOR

Practical Theology in verse Vol. 1

Practical Theology in verse Vol. 2

Practical Theology in verse Vol. 3

Christmas Poems

Collected Sonnets

Fifty Sonnets for Pentecost

The Strange Story of Samuel Parker Eatwell and other stories in verse

Ebenezer Moneypiece and other poems

A Hymn of Praise for Celtic Saints

KINGS & QUEENS of England 1066-2012

The Normans
William I (1066-1087)
William II (1087-1100)
Henry I (1100-1135)
Stephen (1135-1154)
Matilda (1141)

The Angevins
Henry II (1154-1189)
Richard I (1189-1199)
John (1199-1216)

The Plantagenets
Henry III (1216-1272)
Edward I (1272-1307)
Edward II (1307-1327)
Edward III (1327-1377)
Richard II (1377-1399)

The House of Lancaster
Henry IV (1399-1413)
Henry V (1413-1422)
Henry VI (1422-1471)

The House of York
Edward IV (1471-1483)
Edward V (1483)
Richard III (1483-1485)

The Tudors
Henry VII (1485-1509)
Henry VIII (1509-1547)
Edward VI (1547-1553)
Mary I (1553-1558)
Elizabeth I (1558-1603)

The Stuarts
James I (1603-1625)
Charles I (1625-1649)
The Lord Protector (1649-1660)
Charles II (1660-1685)
James II (1685-1688)
William III and Mary II (1688- 1702, 1688-1694)
Anne (1702-1714)

The House of Hanover
George I (1714-1727)
George II (1727-1760)
George III (1760- 1820)
George IV (1820-1830)
William IV (1830-1837)
Victoria (1837-1901)

The House of Saxe-Coburg-Gotha
Edward VII (1901-1910)

The House of Windsor
George V (1910-1936)
Edward VIII (1936)
George VI (1936-1952)
Elizabeth II (1952-present)

WILLIAM I (1066-1087)

William the Conqueror came to our land,
Bold and courageous, a sword in his hand.
He led a great army of brave men of war,
Who, crossing the channel, invaded our shore.
William was Norman, and lived near the sea,
Which the Lord God created, for you and for me.
If the weather is good, and the sky becomes clear,
From Normandy you can see England is near!
Invited to London in ten fifty one,
The pious King Edward had asked him to come-
This King who was loved and was greatly admired,
Was called the 'Confessor' for he had acquired
Wisdom and holiness, gifts from on high
For wherever he was, God Almighty was nigh!
He spoke kindly with William, and said 'After me,
The King of this realm the Lord wills that you be.'
A month or two later, and during a gale,
A ship that had lost both its rudder and sail
Was wrecked on the rocks of the Normandy shore,
No one was drowned; all were safe and were sure.
Saved from the ocean, and its tides and its waves,
The passengers hid from the storm in the caves.
Among them was Harold, who, covered in mud,
Was one of the passengers saved from the flood.
He was taken to William, who, living nearby,

WILLIAM I (1066-1087)

Gave him some food, and then helped him to dry.
As they stood and they prayed, Harold promised to him
He'd be his true vassal of life and of limb.
Later that year, the Confessor fell ill;
His soul was alive, but his intellect still,
And after some days, as the Psalter was read
By Bishops and monks who surrounded his bed,
He gave up his breath, and quietly he died,
As he gazed on the cross of his Lord crucified.
When Harold had heard the Confessor was dead,
He determined he wanted the crown in his stead.
A council of nobles was called to agree
That Harold, the King of the realm now should be!
Harold, it seems did not worry a lot
For the oath that he'd made, he'd completely forgot,
But William, informed of this treacherous deed,
Instructed a messenger, known for his speed,
To deliver a missive to Harold, who read:
'I have heard', thus wrote William, 'that Edward is dead.
Now you are my vassal, and you promised to be
Of those who are faithful and loyal to me.
You've accepted the crown which is certainly mine,
As proclaimed by the holy confessor divine.'
Then William began to prepare for a war;
He had soldiers and archers and horses in store.
He invited brave warriors and valorous men
To help him defeat this usurper, and then,
With his earls and his barons he certainly planned
How he would rule and distribute the land.

WILLIAM I (1066-1087)

He built many boats, which were solid and strong,
His tactic was simple, and couldn't go wrong.
He sent an archdeacon* to Rome, with success,
And persuaded the Pope it was right he should bless
The armada of ships, which would sail over sea
And conquer that island where William should be
Monarch and King, as Saint Edward proclaimed,
'God bless this endeavour!' the Pontiff exclaimed.
Now Harold had gone to the North once again,
For the Vikings had come, reeking terror and pain,
On entering York he was appalled and surprised
When a messenger came and he was advised
That William had landed at Pevensey Bay;
He marched back to London without a delay.
At Hastings, the Conqueror knew how he should
Deploy all his soldiers, their strategy good,
King Harold was killed, with his horses and men,
And England has not been invaded since then.
Victorious in battle, King William employed
His army, with orders that must be destroyed
The cultural values that England possessed,
Even the wisdom which Edward confessed.
All was replaced by manners uncouth,
Practised by adults, and encouraged in youth.
The rest of his reign he was fighting all those
Who resisted his force, there were many who'd chose
To flee to the forests, where they thought they could be,
Happy and prosperous, peaceful and free.
William decided he wanted to know

*Gilbert, Archdeacon of Lisieux

WILLIAM I (1066-1087)

Who were the landowners, why were they so,
Had they inherited their fields and their farms?
Who were the knights, and which were their arms?
Many the details he carefully took,
And entered them in a remarkable book.
In ten eighty seven, he signed this decree:
'William, my son, will be King after me.'
He fell off a horse, he'd become very stout,
And mortally injured, he gave a great shout.
He died in September, they found in his will
'My wealth must be given to the poor and the ill.
May God give me rest, and forgive me my sins'
And so with King William our book now begins.

WILLIAM II RUFUS (1087-1100)

William the Second is known as a king
Who relished the joy his position could bring.
Feasting and dancing and hunting for deer
Were all that he cared for, and gave him good cheer.
The barons who did not approve were beware,
And knew they must take most particular care,
For William was ruthless, if ever he heard
Someone find fault with him, he was perturbed.
And he'd banish that person away from his court;
His anger was sudden, his temper was short.
Now when he had hunted and killed a wild boar,
He'd find a near castle, and knock on the door.
Feigning surprise, then, the baron would say
'An honour for us is your visit this day!
And now we shall hurry to quickly prepare
A banquet in which we all hope you will share!'
When King William was present, and used to attend
Such revelry, dancing seemed never to end.
His shirts were refined, and perfect his shoes.
He knew the best tailors and them he would use
To make his fine costumes of linen and silk,
His elegant stockings were whiter than milk.
He ignored the advice that his counsellors gave,
And yet he was able to strengthen and save
The kingdom his father had won by the sword,
Although it would seem he was idle and bored.

WILLIAM II RUFUS (1087-1100)

His head of red hair would fly up in the air
As he galloped, pursuing a stag or a hare.
Early one morning, a considerable wind
Blew through the forest,* which hadn't been thinned.
William was taking his early-morn ride,
His horse cantered well, and was fully in stride,
When his hair was caught up in the branch of a tree
And the King was unable to set himself free.
Somebody came, when no one was around,
And shot at the monarch, who fell to the ground.
Pierced through his heart, by an arrow, he died,
Early one morning, while out on a ride!
In Winchester Abbey they laid him to rest,
Of Kings one might say, he was not of the best.

the New Forest.

HENRY I (1100-1135)

William was succeeded by Henry the First,
This son of the Conqueror truly did thirst
For the royal estate, which he fashioned anew;
He understood well what a king ought to do.
The brother of William the Second was wise,
And listened with interest to those who'd advise.
When a messenger told him his brother was dead,
And that he would succeed him and reign in his stead,
He hastened to London and, after three days,
Was crowned King of England. Mysterious the ways
Of Providence, lo! In an hour all can change,
To mortal intelligence sudden, and strange.
He chose a good chancellor, Roger by name,
Bishop of Salisbury, a man without blame.
When Henry was absent, he governed the land,
With a competent, just and merciful hand.
Now Henry decided his court should be seen;
This was not easy and would obviously mean
His courtiers must travel with him through his realm,
A splendid procession, with the King at the helm
He ordered the barons to come once a year
To his court and declare, without trouble or fear,
Their financial estate, they did what he said,
And taxes were paid, sometimes chattels instead.
A cloth that was chequered was always conferred
On who piled up money, few errors occurred,

HENRY I (1100-1135)

And unto this day the Chancellor's called
Of the 'Exchequer' when he is installed.
The King had a son of extraordinary grace,
His bearing was noble and handsome his face.
This beautiful Prince was admired and adored,
And it seemed the succession by him was assured.
Then tragedy struck, when this wonderful son
Went aboard the 'White Ship' and was having some fun
Crossing the sea in the dark of the night,
And found it amusing to be without light.
He was drinking with friends, they were travelling fast,
When the boat struck a rock that they should have gone past.
Panic aboard, for the water was cold,
The ocean was deep; and thus we are told,
He drowned in the sea, and so this was the end
Of this beautiful Prince, on whom much did depend.
Henry then gathered his barons and men,
And obliged them to swear on the Bible that when
He departed this life for the Kingdom above,
And stood before Him who is life and is love,
They'd acknowledge his daughter, Matilda, as Queen,
And thus her accession would be calm and serene.
But when Henry had died, though, they could not agree
Who should succeed him, and alas we shall see
That these barons and nobles declared civil war,
Forgetting completely the oath that they swore.
Henry loved England, of which he was King,
And Normandy seemed less important to him.
At the end of his life, he was certainly sad,
But when he was young, he was happy and glad.

STEPHEN (1135-1154)
MATILDA (1141)

Now Stephen had sworn by an oath to be true
To Matilda his cousin, but he certainly knew
There were barons and earls who rejected the Queen,
And who wouldn't be happy until they had seen
A man on the throne as their Sovereign and Lord,
And for this they were ready to take up the sword.
The bishops, the earls and the barons and men,
Were not of one mind, and immediately when
King Henry was dead, they met and agreed
Their oath was not free, and so who should succeed?
Roger of Salisbury approved and became
Stephen's advisor, supporting his claim.
When informed he was King, Stephen wept and he said,
'Is there no one who's able to rule in my stead?'
He knew very well he was fragile and weak,
Indeed he was shy and so gentle and meek!
In eleven thirty five he was crowned as the King,
And, alas, from that day civil war did begin.
Matilda rebelled; her realm was at stake.
She determined to fight and refused to forsake
The crown and the throne she considered were hers,
Usurped by a man who she said, was perverse.
Stephen was kind, and would never offend
The bishops and barons, on whom he'd depend,

STEPHEN (1135-1154) MATILDA (1141)

His decisions were weak, for he wanted to please,
His friends and his counsellors felt ill at ease.
Chaos, disorder and long civil war
Ruined our country, the sword became law,
Barons and nobles then attacked one another,
And brother took arms and would kill his own brother!
'The Lady of England'* was curt and unkind;
Irksome and rude, she was often inclined,
To govern and rule in an unpleasent way,
Not listening at all to what others might say.
King Stephen was captured, but soon was released.
He was crowned once again, but the fighting increased.

Important it was, and still is today,
For the Sovereign to find the desirable way
To show he is bound to his peoples by love,
As God-who-is-Love, is, on His throne up above.

Slowly but surely did Stephen progress,
And Matilda accepted, in bitter distress,
To leave England's pleasant and beautiful shore,
Her hills and her dales she would see nevermore.
Henry, her son, still fought on, but in vain,
He spent all his money, and soon it was plain,
That neither could win this unfortunate war,
So the earls and the barons agreed to a law:
That Henry be King, on the day Stephen died,
And to this arrangement they gladly complied.

*this was the title that Matilda gave herself

STEPHEN (1135-1154) MATILDA (1141)

Stephen was thus the last Norman to rule;
Kind and forgiving, he wasn't a fool.
His reign though, alas, was in time of unrest,
When many took arms to sincerely contest
His lawful succession; maybe they were right,
But quarrels cannot be resolved by a fight.
And only when humbly we do the Lord's will,
Then hearts will be peaceful, and loving and still.

HENRY II (1154-1189)

Henry was born and brought up during war,
And was sad and dejected whenever he saw
His mother Matilda was fighting in vain
For the crown and the kingdom she'd never obtain.
Mature and quick witted, though just twenty two,
On becoming a King, Henry knew what to do.
A powerful person, energetic and strong,
He'd listen with joy to a troubadour's song.
He dressed like a hunter, his clothes were in green,
And a hawk on his arm then completed the scene.
He could read and could write, and enjoyed a debate
He lacked sense of time, and was early or late!
His memory fine, he remembered a face,
And many years later could describe any place
Where once he had feasted, or slept on a bed,
He paid great attention to all that he said.
Usually tolerant and yet he could be
Angry and cross if one did not agree
As monarch, he'd received special grace and was blessed
With divine right of God, that no one should contest,
For if they were heard to be casting a doubt,
On what the King said, he would cry and would shout.
In all other matters he could argue, persuade,
But to put into question his rights, always made
King Henry dejected. He was sad when at court,
He saw someone's words did not tie with their thought.
A minute's reflection would often suffice,
To questions his answers were short and precise.

HENRY II (1154-1189)

He considered his subjects should always agree
His grandfather 'd been the best king that could be.
Queen Eleonora would always forgive
His many adventures, she knew how to live
In a manner befitting a wife and a queen,
She was patient and modest, and calm and serene.
Henry and Geoffrey, Richard and John
The princes, his sons, never knew where he'd gone,
For Henry decided his sons should not share
In his plans which were often unjust and unfair.
Later the King said 'I'm source of all law,
Only my judgement I know to be sure.'
He spoke with himself, and he lived all alone
And little by little his heart became stone.
His theories were strange, his philosophy too,
The courtiers who worked with him very well knew
Who did not agree with him, fell from his grace,
And would soon disappear to a faraway place.
When he was old he was never content,
His appearance untidy, his hair was unkempt,
And in the last years of his difficult reign
His eldest son Henry rebelled once again.
Sorely defeated, his army undone,
Then Henry, like David, wept over his son!*
Richard and John later captured the King,
Who became quite insane on the first day of spring.
The loss of his mind thus preceded his death;
In mental disorder he gave up his breath.
His eldest son Henry had died of despair,
So his second son Richard the first was his heir.

*2 Samuel 9 v 33

ADDENDUM: KING HENRY II AND ST. THOMAS A BECKET

Saint Thomas was born in eleven eighteen,
As a child he was happy and calm and serene.
His father, a Sheriff of London, was rich,
Noble and honest, those qualities which
A father is happy to see in his son,
Who is serious and good, and a stranger to fun.
Praying in church was his everyday joy,
For this was indeed an exceptional boy.
Thomas was glad when he sat down to learn
And all that he did was done calmly in turn.

When he'd finished his studies at Paris in France,
He settled in London, he had the good chance
To meet the Archbishop, the great Theobold.
The prelate was tired and already was old,
So he asked the young Thomas to work with his staff,
Acting discreetly upon his behalf.
The Bishop thought highly of Thomas, and saw
How important it was that he knew about law.
So Thomas returned to his studies again,
He read and consulted and soon did obtain
A diploma in law, and adroit and astute,
He was known as a scholar of fame and repute.
Ordained as Archdeacon, he met with the King,

ADDENDUM: KING HENRY II AND ST THOMAS BECKET

Who saw the advantage their friendship could bring.
For the newly crowned monarch was starting to search
How he could rule and could govern the Church.
Thomas the monk had a spiritual taste,
He was modest and humble, obedient and chaste.
When talking with Thomas, King Henry was glad,
And when in his presence he never was sad.
Their friendship was true, and they both understood
That law should be just, and be wise and be good.
Henry then issued a royal decree:
Becket, Lord Chancellor now was to be!
But Thomas was humble and careful and wise,
He gave his advice but would not criticise.
For he knew human sentiments change very fast,
God's love for mankind is alone what will last!
Archbishop Theobold fell very sick,
His breathing unusually painful, and quick.
The bishops and priests surrounded his bed,
As prayers for the dying were sung and were said.
King Henry was waiting for Theobold's end,
And prepared in his stead, to place Thomas, his friend.
A letter was brought to the King from the Pope
Great was his joy and fulfilled was his hope,
When Thomas à Becket was ordained and enthroned,
Prayers for his health, and long years were intoned.
Created a Bishop and filled with God's grace,
At Canterbury, Thomas took Theobold's place.
After prayer and reflection he knew that he must
Look after the Church God had put in his trust.

ADDENDUM: KING HENRY II AND ST THOMAS BECKET

Now Henry was sure that his friend would do all
That he asked and requested, but then came the fall.
Thomas Archbishop would not let the King
Change Canon law, for this surely would bring
Disorder and chaos. The Bishop professed
'The Church is the Lord's, as the Council confessed'
Thomas the martyr knew Henry so well,
That seeing him angry, of course he could tell
His career as Archbishop was nearing its end,
For enemy now, who had been his good friend!
Secret and strange is the heart of a man
Which changes so quickly and easily can
Transform human sentiment, love becomes hate,
How sorry and sad is this tragic estate.
'O who will get rid of this meddlesome priest?'
Cried Henry, his hate for the Bishop increased.
Some knights hired a boat and to Canterbury came,
And Thomas, the lamb, by the altar was slain.
Henry regretted this terrible crime,
And during the day he would always find time
To pray for the soul of the Bishop his friend,
Who met such a grievous and terrible end.

RICHARD I LIONHEART (1189-1199)

Richard the First is known to this day
As a king who was absent and always away.
He reigned for ten years, but was six months at home,
He abandoned his subjects and left them alone.
He spoke little English, he hadn't learnt well
And he only had stories of battles to tell.
He had a strange accent no one understood,
Common tradition though, rates him as good.
In eleven eighty nine he was crowned as our King,
The people rejoiced when they heard the bells ring!
Richard immediately raised a crusade;
An army from Europe to come to the aid
Of Christians who live in the land of the Lord*
And free Jesus' tomb by the power of the sword.
A man of great valour, it was certainly then
That his archers and soldiers, and household of men
Shouted: 'Our King has the heart of a lion!'
But he was unable to free Holy Sion.
Returning to England, his boat put ashore,
Damaged by rocks, it could travel no more,
So the King was obliged to continue by land.
Passing through Austria he was faced by a band
Of outlaws who caught him, and sold him for gold
To the miserly King who was called Leopold.

*Palestine, the Holy Land.

RICHARD I LIONHEART (1189-1199)

In England his people asked 'Where has he gone?'
A troubadour found him, and only upon
The payment of ransom, was he free to go home,
Where for some months he could sit on his throne.
Restless in England, he travelled to France,
And there once again with his sword and his lance,
He fought at Limoges, where he fell off his horse,
An arrow had struck him with terrible force.
So Richard the Lionheart was wounded and died,
Whilst fighting for treasure in French countryside.
Exalted by many in poem and song,
Who praise his intention of righting the wrong,
Richard himself used to write and compose
Music he'd sing when he was sad and morose.
God knows the heart and the mind of a man,
And it is certain that only He can
Discern the intentions therein that are found,
Which grow and take root as do seeds in the ground.
Were Richard's ideals both righteous and true?
His military tactics audacious and new?
Can we agree to the methods he used
To kill and destroy? We all are confused,
For this troubadour King would not open his heart,
As soon as he came, he'd prepare to depart!

JOHN (1199-1216)

Queen Eleonora gave birth to a son,
King Henry decided 'His name shall be John'.
This was the day when God-who-loves-men,
Was born in a stable at Beth-lehem.
Wise men who had followed the light of a star,
Who had journeyed from lands and from cities afar,
Were joined by the shepherds, and knelt down before
Him, who in heaven, the angels adore.
So this was a day of much joy for the King,
God's mercy and love, he would silently sing.
This prince newly born was the fourth of four brothers,
He had a firm character like the three others.
Later his brother left England again
To fight at Limoges, and was wounded and slain,
Then John became King, which he didn't expect,
But which for the good of the realm he'd accept.
In the year of one thousand, two hundred and seven,
England was locked by the Pope out of heaven,*
Now John was astute, and pragmatic and wise,
As a good politician, he would exercise
The art of a ruler, with talent and grace,
No sentiment ever appeared on his face.
His desire: That the Church in our island be free,
Directed by bishops he determined should be
Chosen in England, and not from abroad,
Their loyal allegiance would thus be assured.
However, the Pope felt he could not approve.

*all England was excommunicated by the Pope

JOHN (1199-1216)

For if he accepted this law would remove
The Roman authority - this could not be
The Pope and his cardinals all would agree.
The people were worried, for then, at that time
To be locked out of heaven was the sign of a crime.
The King understood this, and changing his mind,
Although in his heart he was not so inclined,
Decided 'twas better to give in to Rome,
Than having anxiety fill every home.
But the real success of this King was to be
A law he agreed to, indeed it was he
Who laid the foundations for what we may call
A form of democracy, freedom for all.
He signed that most famous and great Magna Carta;
An important, essential, historical charter.
Much wisdom and foresight the King did display
When he met with the earls and the barons that day
At Runnymede meadow, where he guaranteed
Rights for his subjects, in word and in deed.
He also decided he must introduce
Measures and weights, for our everyday use.
This, the beginning of commerce we know,
From which modern finance would certainly grow.
He lost all his treasure, which fell in the sea,
He suffered and died of dysentery.
This John was a King who certainly knew
That people will later find out what is true.
Despite his mistakes, he did many good things,
And should be considered as great among kings.

HENRY III (1216-1272)

King Henry the third was a very young boy,
And happy if given a ball or a toy,
When he wore on his head a band of fine gold,
Instead of the crown, which was lost, we are told.
Henry when older, was crowned once again,
In Westminster Abbey, no one could complain
For he had been crowned as the King of this land,
And yet what that meant, he could not understand.
While the King was an infant, someone ruled in his stead,
With a very kind heart, and a brilliant head.
The Regent declared that for him the great charter,
Was law of the land to which all were now partner.
The King had a cousin, and nobody knew
What the kind Regent was going to do,
He considered her dangerous; she'd a claim to the throne,
He ordered she never be left on her own.
She was kept in a castle, and under arrest,
Allowed to see friends if she made the request,
She suffered alone, she was young when she died,
And offered her soul to the King Crucified.
The regent who ruled while the King was so young
Was pure in his heart, and was civil of tongue.
He served the boy faithfully during his youth,
Telling him always what he knew to be truth.
But slander and jealousy never find rest
Destroying those men who are often the best.

HENRY III (1216-1272)

And when the young monarch attained his full age,
Men who were wicked and boiling with rage
Came to the King, and desired and implored,
'Imprison that man, may he have his reward
For stealing our money!' The smith though refused
To put him in chains, and he said ' I'm not used
To shackle good men of such honest repute.
Is there somebody here who can find me dispute?'
The King when he heard this, then signed a decree,
That Hubert de Burgh* be immediately free.
He built many churches and abbeys with taste,
His experienced builders did nothing in haste.
The question of levying taxes arose,
The King did not know what he ought to propose.
The taxes collected no longer were sent,
There was certain disorder, he called parliament.
The barons persuaded their monarch to swear,
He'd uphold all the customs and laws with great care
And Simon de Montfort was elected to be,
The baron whose task was to control and to see
That Henry was true to his oath and his word.
The King though decided that this was absurd,
And, raising an army, he fought Simon, the cost
Of his total defeat, meant in fact that he lost
His power to govern, as well as his lands,
Which Simon de Montfort now took in his hands.
Henry's son Edward could not be content,
When he knew the result of this tragic event.

*the Regent

HENRY III (1216-1272)

He spoke with the barons who did not agree
With Simon's political philosophy
An army of nobles, retainers and men,
Prepared to do battle with Montfort again.
They all were persuaded and perfectly sure
The best they could do was to swiftly restore
The King to his throne; he would guarantee peace,
Then Simon de Montfort's ambitions should cease.
When arming and mounting and joining the fray,
The baron de Montfort said: 'This is the day
That our bodies are Edward's', and indeed that was so
His soldiers beleaguered were chased to and fro.
The battle was fought and Simon was killed,
Prince Edward had archers, all wonderfully skilled.
Now order and peace came again to our land,
And many years later we now understand:
There are two institutions which make us content:
A monarch we love and a wise parliament.
May God now preserve us and pour on us all
The rich and the poor, and the great and the small.
His grace and His mercies! We pray that He give
Our Queen many years, yes, long may she live,
To lead us toward that great Kingdom above
Where life is eternal – to live is to love!

EDWARD I LONGSHANKS (1272-1307)

Edward, called Longshanks because of his height,
Was an excellent ruler, who knew how to fight.
His theory was this: that the King be advised,
And all his prerogatives are exercised
With consent of his subjects, for the good of the realm,
As if in a ship, with himself at the helm!
Regal authority is source of the law,
And law is protection, yes, clearly he saw
The law is the same for the rich, and the poor,
And that equality, he must assure.
The first twenty years of his very long reign
Saw general reform, and Edward could claim
A certain success in foreign affairs,
And soon he was known as a monarch who cares.
Peace and prosperity, all understand,
He truly desired for those in our land.
He was prudent, intelligent, popular too,
And indeed much admired, by more than a few.
His government worked every day, with success,
And many the castles he came to possess.
A modern exchequer, concerned with finance,
Did all that it could to see business advance.
His household was modest, and his courtiers knew
They should always be honest, hardworking and true.
He created a council to help and advise,

EDWARD I LONGSHANKS (1272-1307)

The King chose those men who were clever and wise,
His household would travel wherever he went,
The clerks and the many assistants were meant
To assure the King's business was properly done,
From the light of the dawn to the setting of sun.
Edward decided to pacify Wales,
That country so pleasant, with mountains and dales;
He invented the shires, introduced English law,
He built castles inland and beside the seashore,
And then in one thousand three hundred and one,
To become Prince of Wales he created his son,
He turned toward Scotland, and found when they fought,
Their army was stronger than ever he'd thought
The soldiers were trained, their resolve very strong,
Sharpened by everything Edward did wrong.
Later in life he was very unkind,
He couldn't get Scotland out of his mind.
He grew to be cruel, but was unable to quell
That brave Scottish army that fought him so well.
At the end of his life, he was attacked on all sides,
By the French, by the Scots and his barons besides.
While marching to Scotland to try once again
To subdue and to conquer, he finished his reign.
When nearing Carlisle, he fell ill and he died,
His lofty ambitions were unsatisfied.

EDWARD II (1307-1327)

Edward the Second was not a good king.
All through his life, he would search for one thing:
To revel in pleasure and shameful delight,
Oh, what a sad and deplorable sight!
He never was known to bother at all
About matters of state, be they great, be they small.
He studied the law, without any success,
His tutors quite honestly had to confess.
The Prince showed no interest, and was terribly rude,
His behaviour uncouth and his manners were lewd.
The father himself tried to teach his young son,
And showed him how matters of state should be done
But all of his efforts alas came to nought,
Laughter and pleasure were all that he sought!
Not vicious but foolish, and peevish as well,
Those who had known him reluctantly tell.
So weak was his will that he always would be
In the hands of a person much stronger than he.
He ascended the throne, and was crowned as the King;
For him, and for us, an unfortunate thing.
His favourites were killed, he was obliged to relent
And cede his authority to parliament.
In the midst of disorder, the King had to hide
At the house of a friend who stayed at his side.
The barons declared 'The throne is now free',
For they had obliged him to sign a decree,
By which he relinquished the throne and the crown,
Exalted by birth, he was later cast down,
And then he was killed, what a miserable end,
For a king who was seeking a never-found-friend!

EDWARD III (1327-1377)

At thirteen years old, the third Edward was crowned;
He wasn't a scholar, but his judgements were sound.
His mother was regent, and she ruled in his name,
Advised by her lover, of pitiful fame.
He married Philippa at the age of fourteen,
She was humble and modest – an excellent queen,
But Edward's attention was over the sea,
The King of the French he so wanted to be!
He started a war which would last many years
His men fought with arrows, with swords and with spears.
In one thousand three hundred and forty and six,
Blessed by their banners and by Christ's crucifix,
Edward the Prince and that great English force
Engaged the French army at Crécy. Of course.
The archers from England fought well on that day,
As did all the soldiers who entered the fray.
King Edward, who stood on the crest of a hill,
Praying his warriors should come to no ill
Was proud of his young and so valorous son,
And when it was evident England had won
He praised the great courage his army had shown,
And told them: 'I'm sure that you fought not alone.
The Lord sent his angels to be by your side,
May His Kingdom be blessed, and His Name glorified!'
During this war, the young Prince of Wales
Fought on the hills, in the valleys and dales.
His sallies assured that the battle was won,
His armour was black, and it gleamed in the sun.

EDWARD III (1327-1377)

Where the fighting was thickest, and danger had been,
The Prince in this armour could always be seen.
Two years had passed by, when a tragedy came
Upon our fair island – Black Death was its name.
In towns and in villages everyone died,
Numerous doctors and physicians had tried
To discover the root of this plague and thereby
Save some of the thousands of people who'd die.
No one was able to count all the dead,
A third of all England, historians said!
The King fought the Scots, the Spanish and French,
On horse, or by foot, in a field in a trench.
His courage was legend, indeed he was brave,
And did all he could to protect and to save
The realm that he loved, and had served all his life.
When Philippa died, and he lost his dear wife,
Began the last years of this warrior's reign,
A terrible tragedy struck him again;
His son, the 'Black Prince' he so loved and admired,
Who'd battled and fought and who had inspired
So many brave soldiers to fight for the King,
Died of a sudden, one day in the spring.
The warrior King was distraught and upset,
And soon left this world without any regret.

King Edward III founded the Order of the Garter, which, until today is the highest honour that the Sovereign can bestow. This most noble distinction is granted for exceptional service to the King/Queen and country. Among the recipients the first was the Black Prince. Sir Winston Churchill was thus honoured.

RICHARD II (1377-1399)

At ten years of age, and still yet a child,
Richard, a boy who was tender and mild,
Left his young playmates and nurses behind
To enter the Abbey and suddenly find
He'd become King of England. He valiantly tried
To assume his position. He had as his guide
John, Duke of Gaunt, the regent who ruled
Until the young King had been properly schooled.
This Prince was courageous and, even though young,
He knew very well how to manage his tongue.
The taxes were heavy and people were poor,
And famine indeed was not far from their door.
The peasants decided they'd set themselves free,
And coming to London, they wanted to see
King Richard the Second; they thought he would know
The problems they had, when their corn did not grow.
This crowd of poor people were amazed when they saw
The young King himself, would he alter the law?
He heard their complaints, and he said that he would,
Attend to their problems, as best as he could.
Wat Tyler, came forth, and he said to the King:
'These peasants now greet you and humbly bring
To your noble attention, their sweat and their pain,
They labour and suffer not making a gain!'
'My friends and my subjects, I think you'll agree'
Said the King, 'it is obvious to you and to me

RICHARD II (1377-1399)

That order and law must prevail in this land,
Come now, approach, and please give me your hand.
We cannot go home until we can see,
What change in the law you think there should be.'
Wat Tyler then showed him the points to revise.
The King replied 'Certainly, go and advise,
And tell your companions I'm ready to sign,
Even this day, before I will dine,
The abolition of serfdom, low rent for all land,
And even an amnesty. Please understand
This is an offer which comes from my heart,
If you are agreed, then it's time to depart!'
Wat Tyler, alas, puffed up with success,
Came to the King with insulting address.
The soldiers who, standing around the boy King,
Were scared when they heard such a frightening thing.
They killed this Wat Tyler, and all went amiss.
The crowd became dangerous and, when he saw this
The King on his horse cried aloud 'Follow me!',
And all of those peasants, like waves on the sea,
Ran after the King; they would go where he please.
After a time they were tired, and with ease
Were surrounded and promptly sent back to their town,
This was indeed a success for the Crown.
Richard was given two counsellors who
Were to constrain and to limit all that he might do,
For the King was now growing, no longer a child,
Advancing in age, unpredictably wild.

RICHARD II (1377-1399)

He insulted the peers and the earls of his court,
He tried to fight Scotland, but this came to nought.
His critics demanded he dismiss de la Pole,
Who had the young King under daily control.
They'd have him impeached as a treacherous man,
Which he was not - but one easily can
Understand that the courtiers knew not what to do,
For this situation was certainly new!
Some saw they no longer could work with the King,
Some, like la Pole, would do everything
That Richard desired, civil war seemed at hand,
The kingdom was shaking, as if upon sand!
Then two noble barons* who hated each other,
Were banished by Richard, who then used his power
To seize their possessions, he now was a king
Who controlled everybody, and knew everything!
In fact, he'd become a capricious dictator,
And he who opposed him he saw as a traitor.
He travelled to Ireland, and he was abroad
When Bolingbroke,** widely admired and adored,
Invaded the country, and soon became King.
When Richard came back, he could not do a thing.
He abandoned his realm and his royal estate,
He was put into prison, and there did await
A miserable end, for he died all alone,
While Henry had taken the crown and the throne.

*Henry Bolingbroke and Thomas Mowbray, Duke of Norfolk   **King Henry IV

HENRY IV (1399-1413)

Parliament decided that Henry was King.
This wasn't a strange or extraordinary thing,
His father, a son of King Edward the Third
Had been Richard's regent, and people preferred
A king, they believed, who could guarantee peace,
And cause all unrest and disturbance to cease.
But this was not so, for without any doubt,
A usurper was Henry, and therefore throughout
The length of his reign during day or by night,
He was always in arms, and expecting a fight.
Henry was restless, and never at ease,
Courageous in battle, which didn't displease,
But the wealthy and rich who had championed his cause,
And met him with joy when he came to our shores,
Soon turned against him; they expected that he
Would increase their great fortunes, but this would not be.
Rebellion in Wales led by Owen Glendower,
Stretched to the limit his military power,
King Henry the Fourth was unable to quell
The people of Wales, who fought very well.
Glendower their chief, met with great Henry Percy,
Who was known to be ruthless and never show mercy
On those who'd oppose his ambition for power,
This meeting no doubt hastened Henry's last hour,
He suffered it seems, and was always in pain,
He realized glory is passing and vain.
And tired, unsuccessful he lay on his bed,
An hour or two later they discovered him dead.

HENRY V (1413-1422)

Famous and brilliant as a leader of men,
When Henry the Fifth became King, he was then
Courageous and handsome, gallant, admired,
By all the young ladies, in whom he inspired
Romantic, impossible, amorous dreams,
Kindly remembered by history, it seems.
When the usurper had stolen the throne,
He was artful and cunning, his heart was of stone.
His son became Prince, and he honoured his king,
And after his victories, God's praises he'd sing.
As King Henry the Fifth, he fought and he won,
After consulting and planning was done,
The most famous of battles which England has known,
At Agincourt, where the French army was shown
To be fickle, disorganised, for on that day
They were roundly defeated and chased far away.
This victory inspired William Shakespeare to write
His play about Henry, in which we delight.
In just a few years, he took areas of France
Which he organised well, and reformed their finance.
He married a charming and clever princess
This was the summit of romantic success.
Catherine de Valois, who gave him a boy,
To his very great pleasure, and ineffable joy.
Uniting the nation, applying the law,
Who could imagine, yes, no one foresaw
At the peak of his glory, he suddenly died,
A legendary hero, and national pride!

HENRY VI
(1422-1461 & 1470-1471)

Henry the Sixth was King from his birth,
Painful the years that he spent on this earth.
His father, King Henry, had signed a decree:
In event of his death, his son's tutor should be
Richard of Warwick, a man of repute,
Who was peaceful and calm, and avoided dispute.
He made for his ward a library and school,
To read and to write was his everyday rule.
He taught him good manners, and told him to be
Patient and kind with less favoured than he.
At seven years old he was crowned as our King,
Which led to a truly remarkable thing;
This child then of seven, who reigned in this isle,
Was taken to Paris, and after a while
Was crowned King of France; how could he fulfil
His duty as sovereign, when he was still
A child in the nursery, playing with toys,
Like all other healthy and fortunate boys?
He learned by himself to behave like a king,
Although of his duties he knew not a thing!
Now Warwick, as regent, had ruled with success,
But England's interests seemed not to progress.
The King's uncle, called Humphrey, at home and abroad
Caused mischief and trouble with tongue and with sword.
When Henry was young, only fourteen years old,
He recoiled from all bloodshed, so we are told,

HENRY VI (1422-1461 & 1470-1471)

He stayed executions, saved many from death,
Minutes before they would breathe their last breath.
The experienced advisors he trusted had died
So he chose for himself a most beautiful bride;
Margaret from France became his young Queen.
Henry tried vainly to keep peace between
England and France, but he did not succeed.
He was holy, and pious, but direly in need
Of men who were wise, and were just in God's sight,
For he'd never stand up and engage in a fight!
Quite unpredictable, Henry was heard
To murmur and mutter, what he said was absurd.
Chaos, disorder, his depression would bring,
Collapse of the state, in the place of the King,
The council decided to choose a 'protector',
Preserving the realm, and becoming director
Of government policy, he'd continue until
The King was considered no more to be ill.
Richard of York governed England a year,
When the King ruled again, but disorder was near,
Known to us all as the War of the Rose
Henry imprisoned, and we can suppose,
Bullied and threatened, he had to agree
That Edward of York his successor must be.
After battles and quarrels, the King lost his throne,
Edward made sovereign, while Henry alone
Was captured, imprisoned and kept in the tower*,
And there he was killed - how sad his last hour.
This King was so gentle and honest and kind,
His mighty position affected his mind!

*the Tower of London

EDWARD IV
(1461-1470 / 1471-1483)

Another young King now ascended the throne
His beautiful features were very well known
Courageous in heart and wise in his mind
He fought well in battle, in peace he was kind
His face was attractive, his body was strong,
He supported the right, and opposed what was wrong
His diet was varied, he was happy to eat
Rabbits and Pheasants with pies of mince-meat.
The women of London would dream if they could
Of this handsome young king, who was remarkably good
At seducing young ladies! He used to employ
His royal position for amusement and joy.
But when it was needed, he knew how to act,
He studied state papers, and gave orders with tact.
He knew who were friends, and perceived who was foe,
Many would come and many would go.
He married in secret Elizabeth Grey,
Not caring at all what his courtiers would say.

This lady loved money, which she spent to procure
And arrange noble parties of which she was sure.
But this activity often offends,
And Elizabeth Grey lost the best of her friends.

EDWARD IV (1461-1470 // 1471-1483)

Among them Lord Warwick, who'd placed on the throne
Her husband King Edward, he wasn't alone.
The court became sick with ambition and hate,
With plotting and scheming instead of debate!
The King had a brother called George Duke of Clarence
Who said of the Queen: 'I can't suffer her presence,'
Warwick and Clarence took refuge abroad*
The King then believed that his throne was assured!
However these family problems persisted,
And alas, it would seem that in fact they consisted
Of plots and intrigues which Clarence fermented
And only the death of this plotter**contented
King Edward, and also his brother of Gloucester***,
Who considered that George was a simple imposter!
At the end of his reign Edward governed alone,
This was made possible for he was known
To manoeuvre his courtiers with grace and with charm,
Which was indeed his invincible arm.
Was he a tyrant? Maybe this was so,
But who he was really, we never shall know****
When he died, his two children were hidden away,
'To make sure they are safe!' as their uncle would say.

*   in France
** Drowned in a butt of Malmsey wine
*** the future King Richard III
**** the two 'Princes in the Tower'

Edward was born at Rouen in France in the year 1442. Nine months before he was born, his father, Richard Duke of York was far away doing battle, and was absent for a considerable period. This has led some contemporary historians to doubt his royal conception.

EDWARD V (1483)

Edward the fifth, son of Edward the fourth,
Was living in Ludlow, from where he set forth
For London, and there to be crowned as the King,
But death was the crown that was waiting for him!
This joyful procession as it went on its way,
Advancing majestically day after day
Was joined by the agents his uncle had hired,
To furnish a list that he greatly desired
Of supporters and all who would serve the new King,
But death to them all, their intention would bring!
This King was a child of just thirteen years old,
An intelligent boy, we have always been told,
He was happy to meet his Protector and friend,
And God alone knew how this journey would end.
His Protector was Richard, and many might say
He wanted the throne without any delay
For when they arrived amidst ringing of bells,
He said to the youth: 'A young king always dwells
In apartments prepared for him, safe in the Tower.'
His brother was brought there, but who had the power,
To imprison these boys? Their uncle alone,
Who announced he'd adjourn and even postpone
The crowning of Edward, and no one could say,
The reasons invoked to explain this delay.
Were they imprisoned? And can we be sure
That Richard of Gloucester killed infants so pure?
They were seen in the tower – then silence complete,
Where were those Princes, so young and so sweet?
Parliament said: The have both disappeared
Richard is King! People clapped and they cheered!

RICHARD III (1483-1485)

King Richard the third is a mystery for all,
Why did he rise? And why did he fall?
Was he a prophet, a guide, a reformer,
Or did he conceive and commit cruel murder?
Was he disgraceful from the day he was born?
And did he initiate legal reform?
Was he a patriot, defending the nation?
Did he renew the administration?
Brilliant and clever, did he organize well?
History alone will be able to tell!
Was he ambitious, and ruthless and bad?
Did causing distress make him happy and glad?
Was his belief in a God who is love,
Whose cross is the key to His garden above?
Was he a warrior, intrepid and brave?
How did he speak? And whom did he save?
Is it true that he listened to Mass every day,
That he rose up at midnight to watch and to pray?
He reigned for two years, then by permission divine,
His royal authority knowing decline,
At Boswell he lost both his life and his crown,
During the battle a sword cut him down!
His ashes are buried; his bones are at rest,
And no doubt who he was will become manifest.
From the blood of that field, a new England will rise,
Modern and mighty, and glorious and wise,
To build a great nation, and keep the world free,
To the door of the future, the past has the key.

HENRY VII (1485-1509)

His father had died before he was born,
His mother was gentle and sad and forlorn,
She never imagined her son would be King,
For her, this was quite an extraordinary thing!
As the boy grew in age, his guardian knew well
It was dangerous for Henry in England to dwell
So to flee from King Richard, and stay out of sight
He embarked on a boat in the dark of the night,
And with the Lord Pembroke he sailed over sea,
And came to fair Brittany where he was free
To gather an army, and soon he had planned,
How he would come and deliver our land
From the tyrannous reign of King Richard the third,
The crown on a Tudor would then be conferred.
At Bosworth, near Leicester, a battle was fought,
And Henry obtained there the throne that he sought,
His conscience though pricked him, 'til the day that he died,
He was a usurper, that can't be denied!

HENRY VIII (1509-1545)

Henry the eighth then succeeded the throne
With a manner unique and a style of his own,
A man of much learning, versed in Latin and Greek,
New theories and doctrines he'd constantly seek.
Handsome and charming, athletic and strong,
Alas, he did plenty of things that were wrong.
He was crowned as the King and the people were glad,
With him things were jovial, no one was sad,
He studied theology, which he knew well,
And listened to music, as historians tell.
God gave him a mind that was nimble and quick,
He had excellent health, for he rarely was sick.
Arthur, his brother, had been 'highly strung'
And had died when Henry and he were still young
So Henry wed Catherine, his widow and she
Was a Spanish princess from far over the sea.
God is so good and so wondrous and wise,
His ways not perceived, neither seen by our eyes!
Marriage was then a political arm,
And did not depend upon beauty and charm
But rather on sure diplomatic success,
Gained by uniting a Prince and Princess.
King Henry appointed a great man of state,
A man who was clever, and quick in debate,
Cardinal Wolsey from Ipswich, who won
The King's admiration for work he had done,

HENRY VIII (1509-1545)

Persuading the court that this wedding was sure,
And the King with the Queen would rejoice evermore!
Henry's keen interest were books that he read,
Written by authors, some living some dead,
They said that sometimes he would look out to sea,
Amazed by the force of the waves he could see.
The ocean is hiding all manner of life
If the sky be a husband, the sea is his wife!
Affected by tempests and storms from the north
By the gales and winds and the rain pouring forth
Moved by the tides from the east and the west
And the breeze from the south, it is never at rest.
As he gazed on the ocean, what had he in mind?
This King who appeared to be gallant and kind
An important event of his reign was to be
At the Field of Gold, when Wolsey and he
Met the French King, to negotiate peace,
They enjoyed themselves greatly, and talked without cease!
And all those who came and who saw such a sight,
Were amazed and astonished, and returned in delight
For this was the summit of glory on earth,
The gold that was used had immeasurable worth!
When talking with Francis*, King Henry revealed
His clever diplomacy - friendship was sealed.
All that he did, he did very well,
Henry was popular, historians tell.
But he was preoccupied during his reign,
By a thought which would cause him ineffable pain,
For Henry now suffered a mental obsession:

*the King of France

HENRY VIII (1509-1545)

He wanted a son to assure his succession.
Catherine of Aragon had only one child,
Mary-who- never- was- known- to- have- smiled.
Henry decided he ought to divorce,
So he tried to manoeuvre, to oblige, or to force
Pope Clement in Rome to enact a decree,
Annulling his marriage, so he would be free
To marry again, and to father a son,
But how could this action be legally done?
Even the Cardinal could not obtain
His sovereign's divorce, all effort was vain,
And soon it was clear he could not fulfil
What Henry decided was Gods' holy will.
The Sovereign declared: 'I'm no subject of Rome,
I am King of this country, I govern alone!'
King Henry became thus the head of the Church,
The solution he found after months of research.
His Chancellor Cromwell, who did all he could
To obey the king's orders, as chancellors should,
Assembled the members of Parliament who
Agreed with King Henry's new Protestant view.
Monasteries closed, and chapels burnt down,
Their moneys and treasures transferred to the Crown,
The King then announced: I'm now Governor Supreme
By act passed in Parliament - what did that mean?
As head of the Church, he could do as he will,
And those who opposed he would torture and kill!
The result of the act which the Parliament made,

HENRY VIII (1509-1545)

Caused many to ponder, who, sad and dismayed
Could never agree to this change in the law,
Among them the just and the great Thomas More,
'And so let the King' he said 'cut off my head,
I'll follow my conscience until I am dead!'
There appeared a young lady who besotted the King,
Never before had one seen such a thing
The King became young again, seemed not to tire,
His heart, when he saw her, became such as fire.
'Nothing,' said Henry 'can spoil our love
Anne is a gift I received from above.'
His marriage with Catherine was promptly dissolved,
This he considered a sin, now absolved,
Without a delay the King married Anne,
And considered himself a most fortunate man,
Proud of his charming and beautiful wife,
The greatest mistake he would make in his life!
They married in secret, and later that year,
When Henry was joyful, in excellent cheer,
Anne became Queen, but love did not last,
Her fall was as sudden, as deep and as fast
As had been her ascension. She began to displease,
With her smiles and her kisses, she seemed ill at ease.
A daughter was born, Henry needed a son,
And would never be happy until this was done.
As often occurs with excessive desire,
Which burns itself out, like a funeral pyre.
When pleasure is finished and commerce is stale.

HENRY VIII (1509-1545)

Love is no more and marriage is frail!
And so this Queen Anne knew a bitter disgrace,
King Henry no longer would look on her face.
Accused of adultery with a young man,
She tried to defend herself - tell me who can
In such partial conditions, hope they will be
Tried with a justice that's true and is free?
Anne was found guilty, of course, with another,
They even condemned her kind, innocent brother!

-o-o-o-o-o-o-o-

Because we can love, we also can hate,
Like Salomé, claiming St John* on a plate
Many the tyrants who make fun of the meek,
Slandering those who've decided to seek
For all that is pure, and is good and is kind,
Filling with love both their heart and their mind!

-o-o-o-o-o-o-o-

Anne was condemned, and her lover as well,
And even her brother, as documents tell,
They were all put to death, as the King had required,
For the court had to find as the Monarch desired.
Catherine** had died, and so the King thought
He'd marry again, and obtain what he sought***.
He found Lady Seymour, and this was the wife,
He'd keep in his heart for the rest of his life.
Meanwhile the Archbishop had signed a decree

*Mark 6 vv 24-28   ** *Catherine of Aragon*   *** *A Son*

HENRY VIII (1509-1545)

Declaring therein that the King Henry was free
To contract a marriage with whom he desired.
In a very short time then, the King had acquired
The absolute certainty Jane was the one
Who he should marry, and she'd give him a son.
Later he stood at a church in Whitehall
And thanking the Lord, he came forth from his stall
He'd married Jane Seymour, who'd given birth to a boy.
Henry was glad, but his evident joy
Was tempered by sadness, for the mother had died,
Giving life through her death, as the Lord crucified.
Soon the obedient Archbishop arrived,
Thanking the Lord that the infant survived,
And Henry's successor was duly baptized,
His desire for an heir had now been realized.
Jane Seymour loved Henry and he loved her too
Of all of his wives and the ladies he knew
Alone it was she who had room in his heart,
The King was distraught as he saw her depart*
Henry decided to find a new wife,
A faithful companion for the rest of his life.
Holbein the painter had spent a few days
Painting a portrait, which everyone says
Made beauty appear, where beauty was not.
The Princess of Cleves cannot soon be forgot,
Of women the ugliest of ugly was she
And suitors who met her would turn back and flee!
The picture was beautiful, Henry obsessed,
By a portrait he gazed on, and which he possessed.

*Queen Jane Seymour died in childbirth

HENRY VIII (1509-1545)

But of course when he saw her, he reeled in disgust!
And learned that in paintings one never should trust.
He sent her away – 'Do not come here again!'
Shouted the King, and now it was plain,
A divorce was required, which this time he obtained
And without a companion or wife he remained.
Amongst the fair women who came to his court,
The King quite sincerely and logically thought
He'd find the right lady, and make her his bride,
She would love him and help him, and live at his side.
But alas, the young lady who captured his heart
Called Catherine Howard, was versed in the art
Of deception, for while she was sharing the bed
With Henry her husband - somebody said:
She continues to meet with her friend and her lover.
The King would not share his young wife with another,
So he was upset at this secret affair.
He wept bitter tears, and he pulled at his hair,
'How I regret my ill luck with these wives,
All badly conditioned, the latest one thrives
On secrets she hides from her King and her friend,
Such wicked behaviour must be put to an end!'
Catherine and Culpeper* soon lost their lives,
Henry beheaded thus two of his wives.
This King was indeed a man of extremes
Constantly searching for love, so it seems
He never once said: 'I know how to forgive!'
Nor was he sure, somehow, how he should live.

Thomas Culpeper was Catherine Howard's lover

HENRY VIII (1509-1545)

A scholarly man, he was clever, well read,
And an excellent diplomat, as we have said.
Handsome when young, with his sceptre and crown,
He'd change very quickly from smile to a frown.
Today it is difficult to judge him, although
One thing is certain, historians know,.
His father had obtained England's crown by a fight,
Not by succession, but military might,
And maybe it's this which can somehow explain
The anxiety he felt yet again and again.
King Henry was proud of his beautiful son,
And all the child did was most perfectly done,
The King adored Edward, who quickly became
His preoccupation – Oh! Blessed be God's Name!
The court had rejoiced, the news travelled fast,
'The King has a son, and is happy at last!'
They prayed that protected, and filled with God's grace,
This boy might rejoice in the light of His face.
Henry had daughters, as well as his son,
And needed a wife, for now he had none,
He looked around carefully, not very far,
And saw a good widow called Catherine Parr.
He decided that she was the wife he desired,
And the friend and the guide that his children required.
She knew very well he was violent and rude,
Excessive in drink, and excessive in food
But time does its duty and flies away fast
The present and future will soon be the past!

HENRY VIII (1509-1545)

Little by little he became very stout,
His musical voice had turned into a shout.
He was never content, except with his son,
And sincerely regretted that he only had one!
His body was weak and he always felt hot,
His feet used to swell, and he sweated a lot,
And when it was clear that he wouldn't live long,
Though his mind was untroubled, and his will very strong,
He created a council of reliable men
Who were faithful and wise, and he asked them that when
Young Edward would reign, they would act in his name -
Then gently this king of notorious fame,
Lay down on his bed and cried out and died
Archbishop Cranmer said prayers at his side.

EDWARD VI (1545-1553)

Edward succeeded when only a boy,
His birth gave our country great pleasure and joy.
He could speak well in Latin, in French and in Greek
He was obedient and clever, modest and meek.
King Henry found tutors, the best that he could,
Who taught the young boy all the lessons they should.
His teacher once wrote 'He can frame pretty Latin'
He was dressed in pure linen and elegant satin.
He went to the chapel and made his devotion,
And read from the Proverbs, then swallowed a potion,
The Doctor had warned 'His health is not good!'
His nurses, who loved him, did all that they could,
They bathed him and dressed him and saw him well fed,
And gazed at him, sleeping in peace on his bed.
The courtiers were worried: 'He might catch a fever,'
This boy was an ardent and pious believer
He prayed very often, kept God in his mind,
And all those who met him were happy to find
A King so polite and so humble and mild,
He seemed to be adult, yet still was a child.
He became very frail, like a ghost or a spirit,
Whatever he did, it was for God that he did it.
He died of consumption at the age of sixteen,
Succeeded by Mary, who then became Queen

MARY I (1553-1558)

This noble Princess was the child of a King,
How many tears that position would bring!
She wept for her mother through day and through night,
Catherine of Aragon, put out of sight.
Precocious and obstinate, quick in her mind,
Like her father she was cruel, and yet could be kind.
She enjoyed lovely music, and when four years old,
She played on the virginals, so we are told.
When she was young, she started her school,
A Spaniard called Vives established a rule
She should wash in the morning with very cold water,
If you showed her affection, you'd ruin a daughter!
This was the base of that strange education,
Love was forbidden as evil temptation!
When the King had decided that he would divorce,
And spoke of Queen Catherine with anger and force,
He sent Mary to Ludlow, so far, far away,
Where she would live for a very long stay,
She was far from the mother she loved and adored,
Who she knew might be killed any day by the sword,
She hated Queen Anne, who had taken the place
Of her mother, who'd fallen in sudden disgrace.
Mary was happy, as we quite understand,
With lovely Jane Seymour, and accepted the hand
The new Queen had proffered. When Mary was young
She had learned the importance of controlling her tongue.

MARY I (1553-1558)

At twenty years old, with a mind of her own,
She would not accept that a king on the throne
Should be head of the Church. She had suffered so much
When Henry, a despot, and known to be such,
As Head of the Church said he'd not wed her mother -
This was his judgement, there could be no other!
Poor Mary now lived in much peril and danger
Her father ignored her, she'd become like a stranger.
Now Cromwell the Chancellor said he'd agree
To see Princess Mary, and advise her to be
Diplomatic and supple and clever and wise,
Then she'd have favour again in the eyes
Of her ill-tempered father – yes, he told her to say:
I submit to you always whatever the day,
And I promise that now this will always be so,
I accept your decisions, and lie at your toe,
And I faithfully say to my Lord and my King,
I pray now accept this short message I bring,
To work in your chamber as maid is success,
More glorious indeed than to be a Princess!
Summoned to court, the King questioned her: Why
With her father's opinions she would not comply?
She gave him the letter that Cromwell prepared,
And when he had read it, her father declared:
'My daughter, beloved, and jewel of my crown,
Approach me, and look neither up, neither down,
Come now, I pray you, yes, come live with me,
I ask and beseech you to say you'll agree!'

MARY I (1553-1558)

King Henry's sixth marriage was not a surprise,
For Catherine Parr was remarkably wise,
The sisters, she said, should now live with the King,
For parents and children, an ordinary thing.
When their brother was born, they would always obey
To him who would be their Lord Sovereign one day.
Now Catherine Parr took these girls to her heart,
And consoled and advised them till Henry depart.*
When Edward succeeded, his sister was wise,
She lived outside London until his demise,
When the day came, and she mounted the throne,
Mary was virgin, still living alone,
Who would she marry? King Philip of Spain!
No doubt she remembered her mother again.**
Many in England were appalled at the news,
Not sharing at all her political of views.
Mary was always afraid of a plot,
And all through her life she never forgot
The spies and the agents her father employed
When he ordered the Queen come-from-Spain be destroyed.
No proof of a plot against Mary was found -
Wherever she went, she had 'guards' all around.
Her sister was held in that menacing tower,
Then Mary, by virtue of right regal power,
Sent her to live in a house far away,
Called Woodstock, she rode and she studied all day.
At Winchester Philip and Mary were married,
It is commonly thought that the Queen had miscarried.

*Died   **Queen Catherine of Aragon came from Spain

MARY I (1553-1558)

No children were born, this union was sad,
When Philip left England, the English were glad!
Parliament met and refused to accept
A Spaniard as King, and this seemed to affect
Queen Mary, who thought that the Protestant laws
Which her father had signed were surely the cause
Why England rejected the man that she chose,
She decided she'd burn and destroy all of those
Who'd accepted her father as head of the Church.
She ordered her agents to seek and to search
And imprison those Protestant men she despised.
Many good people were shocked and surprised
That where should be love, understanding and peace,
Torture and burning were on the increase!
They considered responsible Cardinal Pole,
Who played at that time an unfortunate role.
When Calais* was lost, Queen Mary was ill
Of a heart that was broken, for tragedies fill
The life of this Queen-who-never-knew-love,
We pray she find mercy in Heaven above

*the last English land in France

ELIZABETH I (1558-1603)

When Elizabeth heard that her reign had begun
She asked straight away that a psalm should be sung,
'All the Lord does is a wondrous surprise,
His ways most mysterious, His judgements are wise!'
Bonfires were lit, as all offered their praise,
For God is Almighty, and Love He portrays!
All over England, the English were glad,
The death of Queen Mary left nobody sad.
While still yet an infant, deprived of her mother
And thus of that love which can come from no other,
She learned very young and alas, understood
That the father she adored and considered so good
Had ordered her mother be killed at the tower -
What a sad use of his absolute power!
She was given a tutor, Catherine Champerowne,
A kind and good lady, and solid as stone,
Elizabeth loved her and day after day,
Would listen politely, and promptly obey.
The Princess was clever, and learned very fast
This good education could not be surpassed.
When King Henry had married the kind Lady Parr
She told him his children were living too far
Away from their father, she insisted he should
See them more often, she knew that he could.
Elizabeth liked Catherine, her father's last wife
Who tried to be guide to her during her life.

ELIZABETH I (1558-1603)

Now when Queen Elizabeth started her reign,
She told her advisors she considered it vain
To impose a religion on men who are free,
Created by God who is One, yet is Three.
She searched for a way that was pleasing to all,
To the rich and the poor, to the great and the small
So that all be in peace as they stand before Him
Who sits on a throne of six-winged Seraphim.
The Queen, who was shrewd, recognized that she must
Have servants in whom she could totally trust.
Amongst them Lord Cecil, who's known to this day,
For the clever and very intelligent way
He governed the country, a great man of state,
He knew how to listen, and when to debate.
When Mary of Scotland was chased from her land
And came into England, 'twas Cecil who planned
How the Sovereign should act to avert civil war,
And keep all our enemies far from our shore.
Many explorers would come to her court,
Amongst them was Raleigh, so gallant and short,
He planted a colony in the New Land*
And called it Virginia – all understand
Virginia's the name of the Virgin and Queen,
Honoured in lands where she never had been!
Her ships filled the oceans, the rivers and seas
With their billowing sails, moving forth in the breeze.
Now England was stable and wealthy, admired
As was her Queen, so divinely inspired!

*America

ELIZABETH I (1558-1603)

She laboured all day to keep England in peace
But danger from Spain knew dramatic increase.
When the great and magnificent, mighty armada
Sailing t'ward England and spelling disaster
Came to the Channel, they met the Queen's fleet,
Which harassed them sorely, inflicting defeat,
The British pursued them, and chased them away,
This mighty armada was routed that day
The great 'men 'o war' found they could not turn back
They had to sail north, their ships seemed to lack
That nimble dexterity needed to fight,
Their fleet appeared awkward, the English were light.
Not one foreign soldier set foot on our ground,
The Spanish Armada had to go round
Scotland and Ireland, returning to Spain,
And never would try to invade us again.
Many were those who were hoping to wed
This beautiful Queen, with a crown on her head,
But she was a virgin, and virgin she'd stay,
To her very last breath, on her very last day.
One morn she turned pale, and the doctors who came,
Said she had smallpox - smallpox of ill-fame.
All over England her people said prayer
For everyone loved her, the country did share
Her distress and her pain. She made a great sigh
And at that moment, they thought she would die.
She came back to life though, and after some days
Recovered completely, to God be all praise!

ELIZABETH I (1558-1603)

Soon she was able to step out of bed,
And prayers of thanksgiving were gratefully said.
She attended to matters of state once again,
And continued her glorious, magnificent reign.
And as this dire malady slowly regressed,
The joy of her people was daily expressed.
The Queen, it appears, did not wish to be married
Perhaps she would say: 'The burden I carried
Was such that I could not have shared with another,
For I took in my arms, with God's help, as a mother,
My people I love, who had stolen my heart!'
She told her last Parliament: 'I will depart,
Will ever there sit here before you a queen,
With such fervour and love as in me you have seen
For this beautiful country and glorious land?
Harken, I pray you, and all understand:
Princes will come who'll be clever and wise,
And some will find mercy and grace in God's eyes,
But will there be any more careful than me
To keep England prosperous, mighty and free?

-o-o-o-o-o-o-o-

Today we reply and we say to the Queen,
Yes, such a great love for our land we have seen
In your royal successor, who carries your name:
Our noble Elizabeth, LONG MAY SHE REIGN!

-o-o-o-o-o-o-o-

ELIZABETH I (1558-1603)

Elizabeth never would name a successor,
Nor did she call for a priest or confessor,
Came Christmas, the year sixteen hundred and two,
She appeared to be frail, and with only a few
Of her closest, most trusted of servants, she came
From London to Richmond; she was not the same,
Completely exhausted, she laid on her bed,
And resting in peace, as the Psalter was read,
While her servants around her in sorrow did weep,
Our nation's dear mother fell gently asleep.

JAMES I (1603-1625)

When Queen Elizabeth, people adored,
Departed this world and discovered her Lord,
England awaited a new Scottish king,
Who was King James, and what would he bring?
The son of Queen Mary,* both handsome and tall,
By his accession he united us all,
England and Scotland becoming one realm,
All in one Kingdom, with King James at the helm!
The King was convinced he had God-given grace**
Reflecting the glory and light of His face,
Maybe the greatest success of his reign
Was the Bible translation that carries his name,
Read still in churches, by many, at home,
Protestants, Anglicans, Catholics of Rome.
After two years of his reign in this land,
Some knaves formed a dangerous criminal band,
They prepared to assassinate James when he came
To speak with his Parliament. Fawkes of ill-fame,
Wicked, and cunning, not handsome, but small,
Was found in the cellar at Westminster Hall
With barrels of powder and evil intent,
The death of his sovereign would make him content.
The plot was discovered, the criminals tried,
Found guilty of treason, they suffered and died.
May God crown this King with His life evermore,
As he finds due reward on that Heavenly shore!

*Mary Queen of Scots   **see Basilian Doron

CHARLES I (1625-1649)

Charles was the second of Stuarts to reign,
His years on the throne brought him anguish and pain!
From the very first day he somehow annoyed
And troubled the Parliament, for he employed
A manner distinguished and noble and brave,
Courageous indeed the example he gave.
He encouraged good architects and paid for their work,
As well as great painters who never did shirk
The portraits and pictures the King would command,
Obeying the detail he'd always demand.
The Parliament soon, though, refused to agree
With the taxes he levied, and soon one could see
Their dislike of the Sovereign, and the way that he ruled,
And his theories of Kingship, they just ridiculed.
His misunderstanding of freedom of speech -
He could not 'discuss' but always would 'teach' -
Led the whole country to an armed civil war,
And that is, alas, what His Majesty saw.
For eleven long years the King governed alone,
Laws and decrees came direct from the throne.
Taxes were levied and war was engaged,
While the Parliamentarians were simply outraged!
When at last they were summoned, they continued to be
In complete opposition, to such a degree
That the King came himself to Westminster Hall,
To arrest those five members who'd consistently call

CHARLES I (1625-1649)

For debate and discussion when voting a law,
Which the King disagreed with, as everyone saw.
'The birds flew away' as the King later said,
Charles went to Nottingham, and stood at the head
Of an army which was loyal to King and to Crown,
With the help of Prince Rupert, of fame and renown.
King Charles, it is certain, was not such a man
Who could hear good advice from someone who can
Know what is better, to attack or retreat,
And probably this would explain his defeat.
Cromwell, the Parliament's military chief,
Would never give anyone time for relief.
Convinced that his cause was both just and was true,
He knew quite instinctively what he should do.
They captured the King, whom Parliament tried
Noble, courageous as always, he died*
On a cold winter's day in sixteen forty nine,
Respect for this monarch has known no decline.
Whilst Oliver Cromwell took into his hands
More power than a King ever had in our lands,
He decided he knew what he thought he should be:
Lord Protector of England - who dared disagree?

*executed 30th January 1649 Cromwell had the heads of the
Kings in King Charles' chess set sawn off.

CHARLES II (1660-1685)

The second King Charles was distraught and upset
When he heard of the death that his father had met.
For he loved his dear parents who'd suffered ill-chance,
Charles and his mother, Henrietta of France.
When civil war started, in sixteen forty two,
He knew quite exactly what he wanted to do;
To stay with his father and fight for the King,
Which was a most normal and natural thing.
His father had taught him: Be humble and kind!
These were the virtues he kept in his mind.
Always forgiving and seeking the best
For those who had helped him, or given him rest.
He was still a young man when he first carried arms,
And fought at the castles, and hid in the farms.
His army, defeated at Worcester, he fled,
Through fields and woods, using leaves for a bed,
Dying his hair and changing his clothes,
He escaped out of England – how? Nobody knows.
He went to the Continent, awaiting the day
The people would ask him to come back and stay.
When Oliver Cromwell fell mortally ill,
England was wondering, who could fulfil
The functions and duties as Head of the State?
This opened a national, important debate.
When the 'Protector' was dead, then certain wise men
Implored the good Prince: 'Come to England again!'

CHARLES II (1660-1685)

General Monk was the first to propose
To Parliament, which one may surely suppose,
Regretted the way that their Sovereign had died,
'Now let us unite and no longer divide
I propose' said the General: 'Charles be our King
For a monarch has such an advantage to bring.
Uniting the nation, defending our cause,
He upholds all our customs, our ways and our laws!'
Then large crowds of people happily came
To see their new King, and to cheer and acclaim
This man who was wise and was greatly admired,
For conciliation was an art he'd acquired.
He faced two disasters during his reign,
The first was the plague, which struck once again,
Thousands and thousands of people then died,
All the physicians had obviously tried
The potions they knew which were then close at hand,
But they never were able to quite understand
This terrible malady, all they could do
Was to bury the dead, and alas, not a few!
Then one year later, at night, someone cried:
'London is burning! Come quick! Come outside!'
The flames had attacked houses built out of wood,
The heat was intense so that nobody could
Halt the advance of this terrible blaze,
And all one could do was to weep and to gaze
At the city of London, disappear in a fire,
Consumed and destroyed on a funeral pyre.

CHARLES II (1660-1685)

This city today is a permanent sign
That often this world will consider decline
What is in fact, a new life-giving breath
For death became life, when by death, put to death!*
Many years later the Germans would try
To destroy this great city and many would die,
But London's protected by Peter and Paul
And will stand without fail 'til the judgement of all!
So he who will wander through London today
Should always remember and earnestly pray
For him, who in haste, travelled far from abroad
When the monarchy had been most wisely restored.
He gave an example as Head of the State
Of a King who was good, and who never would hate.
And later 'twas he who would work to restore
The city, which shines in the world evermore,
And where he now rests in that Church** of renown –
Westminster, where he'd accepted the crown!

*The Cross and Resurrection   **Westminster Abbey

JAMES II (1685-1688)

James was the brother of King Charles the restored,
And as a young man he left England aboard
A dinghy, disguised with a wig on his head.
He sailed overseas, to Holland it's said.
With no one to help him, he searched and he found
His sister Queen Mary, their joy did abound!
He was young and intelligent, clever and strong,
With Mary his sister, he didn't stay long.
He became a good soldier, intrepid and brave,
Who would sleep in a barn, or a tree or a cave.
Many years later, he had to be King,
This was for him a most difficult thing.
When he started to reign, he was determined to see
That all of his subjects be perfectly free
To believe as they will, God Almighty is Love,
And love is His law, both below and above!
In my kingdom, he said, there is one obligation,
To live bound together – one realm and one nation.
From Scotland his nephew attacked from the north,
And on the same day young Monmouth set forth
In the south – but their soldiers were soon chased away,
The army was loyal to James on that day.
The Bishop of London, who quite disapproved
Of his Sovereign's intentions, and wholly unmoved,
By any opinion that did not agree
With what he considered was theology,
Invited from Holland the King and the Queen,
King James ran away, and was never more seen!

WILLIAM III (1688-1702) AND MARY II (1688-1694)

This couple were married for reasons of State,
And from Holland, they came, in sixteen eighty eight,
They adroitly avoided disorder and strife
And then reigned together, as husband and wife.
They would speak in their Council each one in their turn,
He was reserved, and we're told taciturn.
But both were intelligent, and had the same goal:
A Kingdom united, preserved as a whole.
An adroit politician and a brilliant man,
William said: 'I'll do what I can.'
When James had left England, the crown and the throne-
He took this decision, it appears all alone-
A few months were needed to well understand
Who was to legally govern the land?
King James had fled England, and this was a fact,
And nobody knew how they ought to react
For he'd left without writing a signed abdication,
Nor was there trace of a short proclamation.
Parliament met, and gravely declared:
The throne of this country shall be equally shared:
William of Orange and Mary his wife,
Will be King and be Queen for the rest of their life.
When Mary had died, then continued as King,
William who was glad, and was happy to bring,
Stability, peace, satisfaction to all,
This decision was reached in the Westminster Hall.
The Sovereigns had promised that they would agree

WILLIAM III (1688-1702) AND MARY II (1688-1694)

To a new Declaration, whereby they would be
Obedient to law in whatever they do,
And work with their Parliament all their reign through.
William and Mary were enthroned and installed
By the will of the people, now this is called
Constitutional Monarchy, and to this day
The Sovereign and Parliament act in this way.
This King and his Queen came from over the sea.
They were civil and competent, people could see
New laws were adopted, now every three years
The House must be summoned, allaying the fears
Of members who feared an incompetent King,
And the sad situations his actions could bring.
Another new Bill which is still to this day
Applied when is needed, without a delay:
The use of the army is enshrined in the law,
Neither King nor the Parliament can any more
Employ the armed forces for personal means,
This law is now binding for Kings and for Queens.
The act called 'of Settlement' decided who could
Succeed to the throne, and applied as it should,
Gives peace and brings harmony to our great nation,
And in times of distress has been proved a salvation!
This act entered history, and well might it be
A living memorial to William, and she
Who faithfully stood by his side every day,
Advising him what he should do and should say.
Queen Mary died young, William sat on the throne,
He lived most discretely, and always alone.

ANNE (1702-1714)

Next in the line of succession was Anne
Who was always in pain, and nobody can
Unto this day, understand what was wrong,
Physically though, she was perfectly strong.
All of her children were stillborn, or died,
Her hopes and desires were not satisfied.
Little by little she became very stout,
Not able to walk, she was carried about,
A system of ropes and of pulleys was made,
Which in the morning, was used by her maid,
Without this invention, she rested in bed,
And there the state papers and letters were read.
She governed with ministers who she could trust,
A person of principle, she told them they must
Act after their conscience, with love for this land,
She was greatly esteemed, as we all understand!
The last of the Stuarts, without sister or brother,
She never became a satisfied mother,
For of the seventeen children she had borne in her womb,
All had preceded her into the tomb.

GEORGE I (1714-1727)

King George came from Hanover over the seas,
It would seem though he really had little to please,
His interests in life were food, horses and women,
He had good kitchen, and his meals were given
By two Turkish servants, both loyal to him,
He had two nice ladies, one fat and one thin.
He decided one day it would be nice to embark
On a scheme to sow turnips and fill up the park!
He hardly spoke English and Walpole would say,
'I'll brush up my Latin, I'll need it today.
I'm off to the Palace to talk with the King,
If I speak with him English, he'd understand not a thing!'
His interest was music, which gave him much pleasure
He considered George Handel a national treasure.
He argued on every occasion he could
With Augustus his son, who he said, was 'no good.'
He discovered his wife had had an affair,
So he put her in prison and kept her in there,
Forbidding his children to visit their mother!
The King and his son could not see one another
Without shouting, insulting and crying abuse,
Their manner unpleasant, and coarse and obtuse.
King George had two crises to face in his reign,
A rebellion in Scotland was fermenting again,
The grandson of James called the Earl of the Mar,
Proclaimed himself King, in the town of Braemar.

GEORGE I (1714-1727)

This rebellion, though, did not last very long,
King Georges had an army, efficient and strong.
The second event which caused pain and much trouble,
Anxiety and distress was the sad 'South Sea Bubble.'
The South Sea was a Bank for financial affairs,
And thousands of people had purchased their shares.
The accounts were not true, and a terrible crash,
Revealed that someone had stolen the cash.
Investors seemed sure that the Germans at court
Were certainly thieves, and no doubt of the sort
Of criminal men who had ruined them all,
Walpole however averted the fall
Of the Crown and the Government, saving the throne,
By his eloquent speaking for which he was known.
Walpole as minister served the King well,
A great politician, as History books tell.
Hanover City, George never forgot,
And as he grew older, he missed it a lot.
He died and no one was sad or perturbed,
Nor anxious nor worried, nor even disturbed!

GEORGE II (1727-1760)

The father he hated so much now was dead,
The second of Hanovers reigned in his stead.
Tall, he was handsome, and graced with good looks,
He studied quite well, and had read many books.
His soldiers concerned him, and caused him to worry,
He said: 'On parade, you never must hurry,
But march altogether at a reasonable pace,
Not trotting, nor running, as if in a race.
Your boots must be clean, and your uniforms too,
The swords must be shining, the guns as if new.'
His second concern was his court etiquette
Many the intricate rules which he set,
He followed them carefully year after year,
And studied them always before he'd appear;
When should he sit, and when should he walk?
And should there be silence, or could the King talk?
All of these questions and others beside,
Bothered him up to the day when he died!
He shared with his father the Hanoverian hate
For his son and his heir, and it's sad to relate,
His son was called Frederick or simply 'Poor Fred',
'We are not his parents' his parents had said.
How can one explain such paternal disgust?
It would seem that the King had a total mistrust
In his heir, whom he utterly loathed and despised,
Making his visitors very surprised.

GEORGE II (1727-1760)

When politicians would go and see Fred,
They'd listen with interest to all that he said.
They could talk through the night, and discuss and debate,
To think of such things made his father irate.
For the King was unhappy and filled with dismay
If in his presence he'd hear anyone say
What was distasteful and sour to his ears,
Reducing him, sometimes, to sighs and to tears.
The King became rude and unpleasant, he'd shout
And often 'twas difficult to know what about,
In fact he was surely unhappy and sad,
To remember his youth would alone make him glad!
Queen Caroline died, he was rendered distraught,
She'd been ill many months, and simply the thought
Of living without her made him sick and depressed.
But this King was courageous, his behaviour expressed
When leading his soldiers; he loved a good fight,
His victory at Dettingen gave him delight.
'Poor Fred' died in seventeen fifty and one,
The King appeared sad at the death of his son.
At the end of his reign everything seemed to go right,
Great had become England's glory and might!

GEORGE III (1760-1820)

As Prince Frederick had died his son became King,
A man who worked hard and to kingship did bring,
Moral integrity, prayer and a will,
Aware of the duty he had to fulfil.
Aged twenty two when he came to the throne,
Of Hanoverian Kings, one can say he alone
Was serious, good and gentle and kind,
Keeping his subjects he served in his mind.
After some days on the throne he proclaimed
He'd encourage all virtue, for he was ashamed
Of his grandfather's court which had wallowed in sin,
Now he determined his reign would begin
Far from impurity, envy and lust,
'The Monarch is someone you know you can trust.'
He would say in good English, which he had acquired
For which he was certainly, justly admired.
He understood politics, directed the nation,
Keeping informed of the administration.
He trusted a friend, who his mother knew well,
Lord Bute was his name, and the King used to tell
This man of his letters and matters of state,
Without his advice, he would not legislate.
His ministers though, were quite discontent,
Grenville quite often would sigh and lament,
But the King had remarked that without his support,
The government terms were unusually short

GEORGE III (1760-1820)

Ministers stayed if Parliament willed.
And if in their speech they were clever and skilled!
The loss of America, a thorn in his side,
That bothered him sorely, for he had to decide
To grant independence to that land far away,
Which is an ally and friend to this day.
King George lost his reason, replaced by his son,
He talked to himself, and he'd walk or he'd run
From chamber to chamber, through day and through night,
Such a spirit or phantom, Oh! What a sad sight!

GEORGE IV (1820-1830)

George had been Regent for quite a few years
But when he was King, many people had fears
His reign would become like a stale pantomime,
Whilst the country experienced a difficult time.
What can we say of the good 'might-have-been'?
As people then knew, and historians have seen,
Some people say he was not very chaste,
Much of his life seemed to be such a waste!
He restored Windsor Castle, and it was he
Who built a pavilion close to the sea.*
He read all the papers he signed with his hand,
And many were those who could not understand,
Why he reprieved many criminals, and late in the night,
The Minister hastened before morning light
To stay executions, this King had a heart
Which was kind, and most sensitive, hidden in part.
Because of the make-believe world he was in,
Reality was always so painful to him.
He reigned for ten years, and as we have seen
He wasn't the King that he well might have been.

*Brighton Pavilion

WILLIAM IV (1830-1837)

King William the fourth was coarse and uncouth,
He'd become a midshipman quite early in youth.
He knew about boats, and things of the sea,
A serious and competent sailor was he.
He loved Mrs Jordan, an actress of fame,
And many their children, Fitzclarence their name.
However, he married a German Princess,
We do not know if that was a success!
When William was told that he now was the King,
He considered this was an agreeable thing!
He gargled two gallons of water a day,
To stay in good health and keep doctors away.
On the very first day of his reign he was seen
Alone in a carriage, without the new Queen,
Dashing through London, a grin on his face,
Galloping at an incredible pace.
If anyone noticed, he'd take off his hat,
And slow down his carriage to have a good chat.
If they wanted a lift, he'd invite them 'on board'
An interesting journey for all was assured!
He was crowned in a quiet and a dignified way,
No parties or banquets were planned for that day.
He reigned seven years; he had a kind heart,
His interest lay in a map or a chart.
He murmured 'the Church' as he lay on his bed,
And two minutes later they found he was dead.

VICTORIA (1837-1901)

When William died, a girl of eighteen
Early one morning was told she was Queen;
Victoria his niece would now sit on the throne,
At once she decided she'd sleep all alone.*
She trusted Lord Melbourne, who continued to rule,
If she was a pupil, then he was the 'school.'
She followed his tastes in theatre and art,
How important his place in Victoria's heart.
Now Melbourne had charm, and took much delight
Advising Victoria to do what was right.
She was crowned and enthroned at the age of nineteen,
And without preparation, she reigned as the Queen.
The joyous festivities lasted some days,
This beautiful monarch set England ablaze!
Soon she had problems, when Melbourne resigned,
She was used to his manners, so gentle and kind,
To succeed him she had to appoint Robert Peel,
A great politician with a will made of steel,
And when Queen Victoria refused to replace
Some ladies of court, she then had to face
Sir Robert, who straight away told her that he
Prime Minister certainly did not want to be.
Recalling Lord Melbourne, she asked him once more
To form a new ministry, for she was sure
Of advice that he gave her, as mentor and friend,
Sad when his government came to its end.

*until she reached the age of 17 her mother insisted on sleeping in the same room

VICTORIA (1837-1901)

People were asking: But who will she wed?
When a Prince came from Germany, and it is said,
She saw and admired him and all through her life
She adored him, becoming his wonderful wife.
Indeed this Prince Albert was charming and kind
A better companion the Queen could not find.
He knew how to speak with her, show what was wrong,
His views were both moral and solid and strong.
He grew to love England, her customs and ways,
And of course for her Sovereign he only had praise!
The Houses of Parliament later agreed
The Queen might declare that she had decreed
Her husband, Prince Albert, 'Prince Consort' be styled,
The new Prince of Wales was Edward, their child.
Albert agreed with 'suppression of vice'
And Victoria considered this certainly 'nice'
He required that their children behave as they should,
And give an example of all that is good.
The Prince made Victoria quite well aware
Of social injustice, for no one took care
Of children who worked through the day and the night
In underground mines, and who rarely saw light.
The Prince told the Queen about industry too,
About cars, about trains, about all that was new.
A government minister, Lord Aberdeen,
Was instructed and asked by the Prince and the Queen,
To establish with France a new treaty of peace,
Sure that our trade with the French would increase.
Victoria announced that herself she would go

VICTORIA (1837-1901)

Across the wide waters to maintain and to show
That England and France should be allies and friends,
Peace and well-being, upon this depends!
And so she decided she'd travel by boat
Dressed in thick clothes and a fur overcoat,
She crossed over the channel and met the French King,
This was in itself a remarkable thing!*
Prince Albert then organized the Great Exhibition
Enhancing the nation's scientific position.
Alas the Prince died, and the Queen was alone,
In mourning she'd look at his face made of stone**.
She later was styled as the Empress of India
By the end of her reign she'd become very popular.
She'd been many years*** on the throne when she died
And will be always considered our national pride.

*   *the first visit abroad of a reigning British monarch since King Henry 8th*
**   *the marble bust of the deceased Prince Consort*
*** *64 years*

EDWARD VII (1901-1910)

King Edward was old when he mounted the throne,
To many this man was completely unknown
He lacked in the nursery the love of a mother,
And thus through his life sought the love of another.
Happy at parties, he was charming and kind,
And beautiful ladies were close to his mind.
Becoming our King, though, he worked without cease
And travelled round Europe, to try to keep peace
Diplomatically doing the best that he could -
Edward was sensitive, gallant and good.
An excellent King after a wonderful Queen,
How very fortunate England has been!

GEORGE V (1910-1936)

When George was a boy he had learnt how to be
A sailor in ships and a man of the sea,
When young, he'd attended a good naval school
Where tough was the life, and strict was the rule,
That College is Dartmouth, and known to this day
As a place where you learn to respect and obey!
He went on two cruises, as far as Japan,
At heart he was always a true sailor man!
Promoted 'Commander,' this grade he had won
In the year eighteen hundred and ninety and one,
His career in the navy alas came to end,
When Albert, his brother and only true friend,
Died of pneumonia - he had to prepare
To inherit the throne, this he did with great care.
His father would share with him papers of state,
And gave him advice – Never make people wait!
His wife Princess Mary was a tower of support,
Sometimes disarming, she said what she thought,
When King Edward had died, and had found up above,
That which he'd searched for – compassion and love -
George became Emperor of India, and King,
Wearing the Crown and a diamond ring
And with prayers and with blessings, he started his reign
Which knew dangers and problems, and anguish and pain!
George went on visits to lands overseas,
When meeting the Kaiser, he felt ill at ease.

GEORGE V (1910-1936)

His reign was a time of upheaval and change,
When things that were new seemed to all very strange,
Such as travel in cars or in railway trains,
Of what was before, very little remains!
The tragic and terrible, sad World War One,
Which Germany lost, and the allies had won,
Created a Europe not imagined before,
Monarchs had gone, and their Empires no more!
How many died in those trenches of mud,
Moistened by gallons of innocent blood?
The King every morning would kneel down to pray
For his troops who were fighting in fields far away.
When peace was declared and the war had been won,
There was government business that had to be done.
To create a new Ireland, where all could agree,
That loyal be the north, whilst the south should be free,
Was painful indeed, but solutions were found,
A Republic declared upon free Irish ground.
During the war, King George took the name
Of that castle he loved, with its chapel of fame,
He called himself Windsor, and unto this day
His closest descendants are known in this way.

EDWARD VIII (1936)

He reigned for some months, and then left for abroad
Ignoring the pain and the sadness he caused.
'I love darling Wallis 'is what the King said,
'It is she that I cherish, and it's she I will wed'
To have Mrs. Simpson in England as Queen,
Is something that simply could never have been.
The better for England, we say to this day,
But sad he decided to leave in this way!

GEORGE VI (1936-1952)

When King Edward decided to abandon and leave
His Crown and his Kingdom, it is hard to believe
The painful, the sad and sincere lamentation
That followed the news of this King's abdication.
His brother called George, then stepped into his place
Filled with the spirit of merciful grace,
His crowning was solemn and destined to be
Broadcast for all by the new BBC
His people could pray with the bishops and peers
And hear him acclaimed with cries and with cheers.
Conditions in Europe at that time were so sad,
The Germans had chosen a man who was mad,
To lead them, and the world, into terrible war,
His army though never invaded our shore.
King George was a valorous head of our nation
And in those dark hours he'd exude inspiration.
Victory announced, and Hitler destroyed,
The national effort was duly employed
To rebuild our cities, our bridges and streets,
Destroyed by the enemy, nothing defeats
Our great British nation, O Lord grant us peace,
May love fill our hearts and, forever, increase!
King George was admired and beloved, for he
Was a man of great courage, as all now agree,
Beside him, the Queen with his daughters who stood,

GEORGE VI (1936-1952)

Always supporting the noble and good!
Close to his people, he knew how to share
Their joys and their sorrows, and offer his prayer.
He died unexpectedly during his sleep,
Causing his people to mourn and to weep.
Faithful King George met his God and his King,
And hearing the choirs of the Angels who sing,
He knelt before Him, Who said: O my friend,
Come! Live in My Palace, where life knows no end.

ELIZABETH II (1952 -)

And now as we come to the end of our book,
We open our eyes and with wonder we look
On she who has served us with wisdom and love,
Inspired and encouraged by God from above,
For a glorious reign, of some sixty long years,
She has shared all our joys, and has dried all our tears.
And so let us now sing with our heart and our voice,
As all of her subjects together rejoice,
Repeating again and again the refrain:

> GOD SAVE OUR GRACIOUS QUEEN
> LONG MAY SHE REIGN!

EPILOGUE

History's not finished, for we do not know
How many more monarchs will come and will go.
Time will continue to search for its end
Eternity, which it will greet as a friend.
For history will cease on that beautiful shore
Where faith and where hope will be needed no more.
There, Life will be Love which forever will last,
And sorrow and pain will be things of the past.
The KING will appear, and all will bow down
And the good and the bad will take off their crown,
To cast it before the Pure-Lamb-Who-Was-Slain,
Who died that through death we might all live again!

Blessed be that Kingdom,
For there we shall sing
And glorify
JESUS
OUR GOD AND OUR KING!
The end and glory be to God

Lightning Source UK Ltd.
Milton Keynes UK
UKOW05f0516101013

218765UK00002B/16/P